THE GOLDEN BOOK OF THE SPIRITUAL SIDE

By
Father John Doe
(Rev. Ralph Pfau)
Author
of
SOBRIETY AND BEYOND
SOBRIETY WITHOUT END

*"PRAYER—the GOLDEN thread that
binds the hearts of men
about the feet of God"*

* * *

Hazelden Publishing
Center City, Minnesota 55012-0176
hazelden.org/bookstore

© 1947 by Hazelden Foundation. First published 1947
by SMT Guild, Inc., Indianapolis. First published by Hazelden 1998
All rights reserved
Printed in the United States of America
No portion of this publication may be
reproduced in any manner without the
written permission of the publisher

ISBN: 978-1-56838-237-1

Imprimatur: PAUL C. SCHULTE
Archbishop of Indianapolis, Jan. 1947

The matter contained in this booklet was originally a series of notes used by the author in giving talks to the various A.A. groups in the middle west. Numerous requests for copies of the talks made it advisable to arrange the notes for printing. They were first published in the Souvenir Retreat Booklet which was distributed at the third annual A.A. Retreat of the Indiana area. Only five hundred were printed and the supply was soon exhausted. Requests for "The Golden Book" continued to come from many sections of the country which made this reprinting of the text advisable. It is humbly offered by the author with the fond and fervent prayer that He Who was so generously made the work possible, may in His Love draw the reader a little closer to Him.

—*The Author*

PRAYER AND MEDITATION

"Sought through prayer and meditation..."

In order to have a clear mind in considering the subject of prayer and meditation, a true concept of the nature of spirituality is paramount. Many have much difficulty with the so-called "spiritual side" of the program, because they have a distorted idea of what is meant by the term "spiritual." To many, such a term conjures up in their minds innumerable prayers, a long face, isolation, inhuman qualities of human association, a retreating gait, somber groanings, and what-have-you. Nothing could be further from the truth, for a truly spiritual person is a saint, and a saint is very human—but one who has built his life and his actions on *God's* will and not his own. Spiritual men and women are happy—they have no conflicts—for their will is trained to be always subject to the will of God. As St. Theresa put it with two pertinent remarks: "A saint sad is a sad saint" and "Lord, deliver me from sour-faced saints." Spiritual men and women are normal, whereas the grotesque figure conjured above is very abnormal. They keep such people locked up. A spiritual person is one who does *what* he has to do, *when* he has to do it, in the *best* way he can do it and who gets the guidance, the strength, and the success from God through humble prayer and meditation. They realize that whether they pray or eat or work or play or sleep, they do it all for the honor and glory of God and thus they praise God in doing His Will.

Some obtain their wrong idea of spirituality and sanctity from the pictures and statues of the saints. In order to denote sanctity, they are usually depicted in a "saintly" pose *but* we should not conclude from this fact that their whole life was consumed in such pose. Do we think for a moment that St. Joseph went around day after day with a lily in one hand and the Christ Child in the other? Or that St. Aloysius spent all of his days on some side altar dressed in cassock and surplice and his hands clasped in prayer? The lily in St. Joseph's hand simply denotes his perpetual chastity; the Christ Child in his arms denotes his role as protector of God's Son. St. Joseph was a carpenter and as such had to work every day to support Mary and Jesus. He had to put up with all the inconveniences of life the same as you and I. He laughed, and wept, and ate, and slept, and talked with friends, and suffered and died—even as you and I. But he did all these things as *God* willed them--and *that* made him a saint.

With this idea of spirituality and sanctity in mind, we can easily understand that even the often used term "spiritual angle" or "spiritual side" is a misnomer. As one outstanding member once remarked, "Spiritual SIDE? The *whole* program is spiritual." And those who decry it or who so naively remark that they can accept *all* of the program *but* the "spiritual side" are woefully ignorant of the meaning of spirituality. Their statement is a contradiction in terms. As a member once remarked to the writer after a long attempt to discredit the "spiritual side," "There is no doubt but that my seven years of sobriety is a miracle." You figure out that one.

Have you ever analyzed the Twelve Steps and eliminated those steps that are spiritual? It is very interesting—let's try it.

1. WE ADMITTED WE WERE POWERLESS OVER ALCOHOL—THAT OUR LIVES HAD BECOME UNMANAGEABLE.

There's nothing spiritual about this admission. Any drunk can truthfully make it. So we will keep this one—we admit we are in a "mess."

2. CAME TO BELIEVE THAT A POWER GREATER THAN OURSELVES COULD RESTORE US TO SANITY.

Came to a belief in God—in spiritual things. If we do not accept the "spiritual side" of the program then we must eliminate this step...

3. MADE A DECISION TO TURN OUR WILL AND OUR LIVES OVER TO THE CARE OF GOD . . .

Here we make a decision to lead a *spiritual* life, a life surrendered to the Will of God...so we must eliminate this step too...

4. MADE A SEARCHING AND FEARLESS MORAL INVENTORY OF OURSELVES . . .

"A *moral* inventory"—morality postulates a law–the *moral* law. Without God and His Commandments we could not have a moral law. We take this inventory in order that we might adjust ourselves to this moral law—which again is to live a spiritual life. So step four is out...

5. ADMITTED TO GOD . . .

There's God again, so that's out...

6. WERE ENTIRELY READY TO HAVE GOD. . .

God...that's out...

7. HUMBLY ASKED HIM. . .

We can't do it if there is no *spiritual* side...we can't use this step, it's spiritual...

8. MADE A LIST OF ALL THE PERSONS WE HAD HARMED AND WERE WILLING TO MAKE AMENDS . . .

Justice and rights...again postulating the law of God...but there's no "spiritual side"...no submission to God's Will and Law...no restitution...no taking of the eighth step....

9. MADE DIRECT AMENDS TO SUCH PEOPLE . . .

A corollary of step eight...emanating from obligations of justice... so we can't use this one...

10. CONTINUED TO TAKE PERSONAL INVENTORY. . . WHEN WRONG . . .

But only a truly spiritual man need pay attention to right and wrong...to morality...to God's Law...so we discard this step also, it's spiritual . . .

11. SOUGHT THROUGH PRAYER AND MEDITATION TO IMPROVE OUR CONSCIOUS CONTACT WITH GOD . . .

This step is loaded with the very essence of spirituality...we could never include it...

12. HAVING HAD A SPIRITUAL EXPERIENCE. . .

Spiritual! There could never be a twelfth step if we deny there is a spiritual side...

Now what have we left of the program after having thrown out all the steps that are spiritual?

WE ADMITTED THAT WE ARE POWERLESS OVER ALCOHOL—THAT OUR LIVES HAD BECOME UNMANAGEABLE!... What a mess! Open the barred gates, Richard!

Therefore, understanding that leading a spiritual life is nothing more nor less than the honest effort to live daily in accordance with the known will of God to the best of our ability, let us proceed to the consideration of the one thing that is the cornerstone of the whole program, the very life fuel of the spiritual life, and the positive unfailing insurance for continued sobriety and happiness. We express this all-important and essential part of the program in the eleventh step: WE SOUGHT THROUGH PRAYER AND MEDITATION TO IMPROVE OUR CONSCIOUS CONTACT WITH GOD AS WE UNDERSTOOD HIM, PRAYING ONLY FOR KNOWLEDGE OF HIS WILL FOR US AND THE POWER TO CARRY THAT OUT.

No one will achieve sobriety and happiness and serenity for long unless he or she honestly practices the eleventh step. Thousands of alcoholics have slipped. But experience proves that *every slip* was preceded by a period of neglect of the eleventh step, by a neglect of honest prayer, by a neglect of humbly asking God for the guidance and the strength to remain sober. The writer has made it a point to ask hundreds of men who had slipped whether they had sincerely prayed on the day they began to drink. Only one answered affirmatively, and he qualified his answer with, "I prayed and I prayed that *God would not let me get hurt* during this drunk!" This is tantamount to no prayer. We can put it down as an indisputable fact that the one who *humbly* and *sincerely* prays *daily for strength and guidance will not slip;* the good Lord will not let that happen.

On the other hand *all things* are possible to the person who prays. No matter in what condition or how entangled one may be in the problems of life; no matter how long or how much a person has drunk to excess; no matter how low such a person has sunk in the quicksands of immorality or mental aberrations, *if a person prays, he or she will recover!* For alcoholism, unhappiness, wrongdoing, self-pity, resentments, conflicts, and all the hosts of things that the alcoholic knows so well *cannot* co-exist with prayer. One will be eliminated—either he or she will stop praying or even the worst of human problems eventually will clear up under the power of God's grace.

There is a story that frequently makes the rounds of the A.A. groups. It is told to exemplify the extreme of self-pity, and goes something like this:

A certain man was feeling so sorry for himself that he was planning suicide. He had decided to jump into the river and end it all. However on his way to the water, while passing through an adjacent meadow he decided that it would not be a bad idea to say a prayer before he consummated his decision. As he knelt down he removed his hat. At that moment a bird was passing above and deposited its "calling-card" in the center of the man's bald pate. Looking up the man exclaimed, "See God, that's what I mean! For other people birds sing!" There the story ends, but I should like to add a corollary: Did the man say the prayer? If he did, I feel certain he did not jump.

History is full of examples of the power of prayer. Tennyson tells us that "More things are wrought by prayer than this world dreams of." If we only realized it, every happy, normal life is the product of prayer. On the contrary every unhappy, abnormal life is the result of the neglect of prayer.

Striking proof of the power of prayer may be seen in the story of the writing of the Constitution of the United States. The founding fathers had spent weeks in discussion, attempting to draw up the articles to be incorporated into the document. Finally, after much wrangling, Benjamin Franklin arose and addressed the assembled statesmen: "I have lived a long time, Sirs, and the longer I live the more convincing proofs I see of this truth: That God governs all the affairs of men. And if a sparrow cannot fall to the ground without His notice, is it possible that an empire can rise without His aid? I believe that without His concurring aid, we shall succeed in this political building no better than the builders of the Tower of Babel. We ourselves shall become a reproach and a byword through future ages." The next day the assembly was opened with a prayer to God for guidance, and the *same day* the Constitution of the U.S., one of the greatest documents on record, was written!

We know from the Scriptures that as long as Moses knelt with his arms outstretched in prayer, the Israelites were victorious, and that when he ceased to pray they were put to rout. Hundreds of such examples could be given to show the power of prayer in governing the lives of people and nations.

One time a man entered a restaurant to eat. Before partaking of his food he humbly bowed his head in prayer. At the adjoining table were some individuals who decided to make fun of him. "Say buddy," one of the crowd remarked, "does everybody where you come from do that before they eat?" "Everybody but the pigs," the man calmly answered, "Pigs don't pray."

In order to even desire to pray we must first have *faith* in God—in His existence and in His omnipotent power. There are some who have trouble here when they come on to the program. One person solved his difficulty in this way: "I would rather be wrong on the side of believing in God and finding after death that there is no God, than *not* believing in God here and then finding after death that there is a God." Very logical, very simple.

They tell the story of the atheist who noticed a little girl reading the Bible on the train. He approached her and cynically queried, "Surely you do not believe all that trash you are reading, do you?"

"Certainly I do," the girl guilelessly replied.

The fable of Adam and Eve?" "Certainly."

"And Cain and Abel?"

"Yes, I do."

"Jonas and the whale?"

"Sure I do."

"Well, how are you going to prove it? I suppose you are going to ask Jonas when you get to heaven?"

"That sounds like a good idea. I think I shall." "And what are you going to do if Jonas isn't there?"

"Well, then you ask him."

If we do *not* believe in God little in life makes sense. Life becomes an endless "Why?" with never an answer. For it is only the acceptance of the Divinity, of God—His mercy, His providence, His power, His Wisdom, etc.—that can satisfactorily explain to man's reasoning powers the problems of life. As we read in the A.A. book: "On one proposition the members of A.A. are strikingly agreed. Everyone of them has gained access to, and believes in, a Power greater than themselves...thousands of men and women flatly declare that since they have come to believe in a Power greater than themselves, there has been a revolutionary change in their way of thinking and living...once confused and baffled by the seeming futility of existence, they will show the underlying reasons why they were making such a heavy going of life. Leaving aside the drink question, they will tell you why living was so unsatisfactory...and when thousands of such men and women are able to say that belief in the presence of God is the most important fact of their life, they present a powerful reason why we should have Faith...for deep down in every man, woman and child is the fundamental idea of God. It may be obscured by pomp, calamity, by worship of other things, but in some form or other it is there. For Faith in God and the miraculous manifestations of His Power in human lives are facts as old as man himself..."

Can we doubt it?

Then think of the plight of the atheist at death. One time such a person died and his co-worker, Pat, came to the wake. As he stood beside the bier he began to laugh. One of the bystanders chided him for laughing in the presence of the dead and asked him why he did such a thing. Pat replied: "I can't help it. Only yesterday Mike was telling me that he didn't believe in a life after death, nor in heaven nor hell, nor in God, and when I see him in all those fine clothes in the coffin, I can't help thinking 'the poor fellow, all dressed up and no place to go.'"

In order to pray well our prayers should have certain qualities to make them effective. In the first place they must be SINCERE. We all have had experience with the "gimme" prayers and prayers backed by a lying promise. "O God, get me out of this mess, and I'll never take another drink!" The big liar—he doesn't really want to quit drinking, he simply doesn't want to get hurt.

A very good way to test the sincerity of our prayers is by analyzing the Lord's Prayer which we say at our meetings. In this prayer we pray:

"Our Father who art in heaven,

Hallowed be Thy Name..."

Are we sincere when we say this? Do we really make an effort on our part to avoid profaning God's Name? Or is this prayer merely words to us? Keep your ears open at the meetings and listen, "Two years ago I was on the -- --drunk in my life!" *Hallowed be Thy Name!*

"Thy Kingdom Come..."

This means that we pray that all men will come to a knowledge of truth, of God; that *His* providence will prosper; that *His* kingdom will come about both on earth and eternally in heaven. And what do we hear? "That new members there, he's another of those—Methodists, or Catholics, or Baptists, or Jews!" *Thy* kingdom come! Are we looking for denominations or sincerity?

"Thy will be done..."

On earth as it is in heaven..."

And then we don't accomplish what we set out to do. We don't get the job, or the raise, or someone crosses us in any one of a thousand ways and we are burned up, resentful, full of self-pity, and if continued, we're drunk. Why, *our* will wasn't done. God's was. If it wasn't God's will it would not have happened, and after all we pray *Thy* will be done, not *my* will be done. Do we *act* as we pray?

Some years ago I attended an anniversary banquet of one of the A.A. groups. After the dinner and talks one of the members sang a song and dedicated it to A.A. The song was "O What a Beautiful Morning, Everything's Going *My* Way." I believe the singer was badly mistaken in his dedication. Certainly his song's theme doesn't fit into A.A. thinking. For, if we would follow through with his thought, many mornings we would moan "O What a Terrible Morning, *Nothing* is Going *My Way!*" That is one of the attitudes that puts us in A.A.—extremes of emotion, elation and self-pity. But now we strive to acquire the middle of the road—serenity no matter what comes along—for "Everything's going *His* Way"—and it always will. *Thy Will be done!"*

"Give us this day our daily bread..."

We pray that God will grant us *sufficient* strength, guidance and blessings to live *today*. Today means twenty-four hours. We don't pray for tomorrow, nor ask the impossible that God will change the past. We pray only for *today*—and for all that is *necessary* to live this *day, with absolute faith* that God will give us what we *need*, but not necessarily what we *want*. Yet how many of us worry and stew about what might happen tomorrow, next month, next year?

"Forgive us our trespasses as we forgive

those who trespass against us..."

We have taken an inventory and found quite a mess for which we had been responsible. We found that we were loaded with faults and failings. We asked God to forgive us, *"as we forgive those* who trespass against us." Then someone hurts us, crosses us, contradicts us and we are so loathe to forgive! How often we want to get even! Isn't it a blessed thing that God does not take us at our word? *"As we forgive."*

"Lead us not *into temptation..."*

We are asking that God preserve us from temptation to wrongdoing. It is understood that *we* shall do our part to avoid, as far as we can, the temptation to drink, etc. Do we? Do we avoid taverns, and places where whiskey flows freely, except when *necessity* (not excuses) takes us there? Do we avoid companions who drink to excess? Or rather do we permit a subconscious desire to rebuild our "ego" lead us to seek such circumstances? Like the gentleman who remarked, "I go into a tavern every day to drink a 'coke' just to prove to *myself* that I won't take a drink of liquor." He did—drink liquor. Remember Peter's proud boast? "Even though all betray you, *I never will."* Had he been humble he would have stayed away from the courtyard—the source of temptation. "Lead us not into temptation"—grant us the grace to avoid the occasions of sin, and we will do the footwork.

"But deliver us from *all* evil."

Not only that which is actually wrong, but *all* evil, all that is not good, all that is not of Thee. Grant us ever to strive to bring our *entire* life in accord with the designs of Thy loving providence and

Thy will. Do we guard against small beginning, thoughts, etc., that might grow into a temptation to sin? "Deliver us from *all* evil.

"Amen," which means "so be it"—may our *actions* follow our words. We are told in the A.A. book, "The spiritual life is not a theory, we must *live* it...*action* is the magic word."

The second quality our prayer should have is CONFIDENCE. We should pray knowing that God is more anxious to hear our prayers than we are to have them heard. Yet how often are we really surprised when our prayers are answered! They tell the story of the man who had a flat tire and, amid curses and epithets, was having much difficulty removing the tire from the rim. At this point a clergyman came along and suggested that perhaps he would have better luck if he tried prayer instead of cursing. "You're a clergyman," the man replied, "How about you trying it?" Whereupon the reverend gentleman said a prayer, put his hands on the tire, and it fell off. "Well, I'll be -- !" cried the clergyman in amazement. The owner of the car smiled wryly to himself.

There should never be any doubt that God wants to and will answer *every* prayer provided we do our part and it be not contrary to His will. And even should our request be contrary to His will, he *will* answer it in another manner. *No prayer ever goes unanswered.* Although Almighty God often refrains for a time in answering our prayers, He does so to make us realize our complete dependence on Him and to teach us patience and constancy.

There was a story on the radio some time ago which was very dramatically illustrative of this point. It told of a certain individual who became very bitter towards Almighty God because a sudden storm had destroyed the entire yield from his grape arbors. In his resentment he often derided the idea of prayer and the fact of God answering prayers. A short time later his wife suddenly became very ill and was rushed to the hospital. The doctors after examining her informed the husband that there was little hope for her life.

He was permitted to see her for a short time before he left the hospital, and her last words, whispered to him with much effort, were: "Pray for me, Jim."

Pray—pray—pray—the word haunted him, but withal it seemed only to deepen his resentment and bitterness. He went home. As he entered the living room his five-year-old boy ran up to him. "Daddy," the lad begged, "Why don't you ask God to bring mommy home?"

"God?" he questioned bitterly. "God's got cotton in His ears!"

"Cotton? What's cotton, daddy?"

"I mean God doesn't hear you. He doesn't answer you."

"He answered my prayers, daddy."

"He answered your prayers? How? You have been asking God for a red scooter for a long time now and haven't got it. If God answered you, what did He say?"

"God said 'No,' daddy"!

There are times, also, when our prayers go unanswered because we do not *do our part*. Instead of not enough confidence, we have 'false confidence' which is nothing more nor less than presumption. They tell the story of the person whose house was burning down. He calmly continued to sit nearby apparently doing nothing. When a passersby asked him why he did not attempt to put out the fire he replied, "I am—I'm praying for rain."

A very good thought to keep in our conscious mind to help us have absolute confidence in God answering our prayers is that primarily God is our *Father*, only secondarily our *Judge*.

The third quality necessary for effective prayer is PERSEVERANCE. It is not sufficient to pray only when danger or temptation is present; to ask once in a while; or to ask for sobriety and then quit praying. We must pray *daily* and *continue* to pray daily. "He who perseveres to the end, he will be saved." Remember the woman in the Gospel story—even apparent direct refusal did not cause her to quit asking. And as a result her prayers were more than answered (Matt. xv; 21-28). Our faith must be such that against all odds we *persevere* in prayer for ultimately our prayer *will* be heard. We must "keep on swimming" like the two little frogs who jumped into the pail of cream. After many futile attempts to get out one gave up and drowned, but the other kept on swimming and finally found that he was sitting on a pail of butter from which he easily jumped to safety.

The fourth quality that our prayers should possess is that they should be DELIBERATE. Remember that prayer is a *two*-way conversation. We not only ask and tell, but we *listen*. Therefore our prayers should not be hurried, and should be free from distractions so that this may be possible. As Christ tells us, "When you pray... pray to the Father in secret," i.e., in the *quiet* of our souls devoid of worldly distractions and problems. Thus and thus alone will we be able to hear the Voice of the Divine Master.

There was once a poor boy who had no shoes. Being a very pious lad, he was taunted one day by a passerby, "You say so many prayers, it seems to me that if God heard them He would tell someone to buy you a pair of shoes."

"Please, mister," the boy answered, "I think He does, but they don't listen."

The most important times for prayer are:

1) IN THE MORNING. It is here that we ask for the strength and the guidance for the day. Many are the ones who fall into sin, because they did not ask God for the strength to avoid wrong; because they did not say their morning prayers; because *they were on their own*. We should keep ever in our conscious mind the *Fact: No one ever slipped who honestly and sincerely asked God that morning to keep him sober that day*. We do not go to town to shop without money with which to make our purchases. Likewise we *cannot* go through the day sober, and serene, and secure *without* the strength of God which is only given to those who ask.

2) IN TIME OF TEMPTATION. When doubtful, agitated, tempted—we should pause and ask for the light, the strength, and the guidance. We should always remember that the *Power of God* is at our disposal at *all* times, and in *all* places, and under *all* circumstances for the *asking*. Did you ever try it?

3) AT NIGHT. All our life we shall remain human and shall be burdened with fallen human nature. From the Scriptures we know that even "the just man falls seven times a day" and that "if any one says that he is without sin, that man is a liar and the truth is not in him." Therefore *each* evening we should ask forgiveness of the faults of that day. We should renew our resolves. We should make up any wrongs. We should *thank* God for having had sobriety and all the

rest of His blessings for another day. The more grateful we are for blessings received, the more blessings will God shower upon us.

It is also a very good practice to have a set time for our prayers. We are far less apt to forget or omit them if we say them at the same time each day. It is good psychology. It gives us something to hang our will onto. On the other hand a general resolution to 'pray every day' seldom proves effective. It is too indefinite.

Now let us consider the matter of MEDITATION. To most people it seems so difficult, yet in reality it is very simple. It is absolutely necessary for living a good life free from doubts and conflicts. Meditation purifies the mind and motivates the will. It is simply the turning over in our minds of a *truth* (any truth) in order that, becoming a conscious factor in our lives, it will motivate our wills to right action. It is the giving truth a 'good think.' Let us take an example; let's meditate a few moments on *death*.

What is death? Death is the end of life on earth, the end of all that I cherish so much now. Then I shall see no more of this world, shall hear no more the voices of my friends and loved ones, shall no longer breathe nor speak nor move.

Who? *I*—that big ego that I now pamper so much—I am going to die!

When? I don't know—next year? Maybe. Next month? Maybe. Tomorrow? Maybe. *Today?* Could be. The startling fact is that I may die at any moment! *I do not know* the day nor the hour, but it could be today!

Where? At home? Away—from friends and loved ones, alone?

By what means? An accident? Disease?

How am I going to die? Sober? Drunk? God forbid, but *many have died drunk!* Shall I die suddenly? Without time to prepare? Without time to ask God's forgiveness? Without time to say a prayer? At peace with God or in sin?

Think—think–think—I am going to die! I cannot know when or where but *I can know how—if—if—I live each day prepared to meet my God.*

Now do you think we could very easily go out and take that first drink? Do you think it will be difficult to try to lead a good life today? Will it be so hard to be faithful to prayer today? Not with those thoughts in our mind. We shall probably the more cry out "O God teach me to pray, so that I may learn to live—and to die." *For as we pray we shall live—and as we live we shall die—therefore if we pray well we shall live well—*and *if we live well we shall die well—and that is all that matters!*

THINK IT OVER!

HUMILITY

*"He hath scattered the proud in the conceit of their heart...
He hath exalted the humble"*

The entire Twelve Steps of A.A. Program are based on humility. Without it there can be no actual *taking* of the twelve steps. For without humility the program would be nothing more nor less than a continuation of a life of sham and hypocrisy. Without it prayer would be only an empty collection of words—ineffective and lifeless, whereas "an *humble* and contrite heart God will not despise." Without it there is no alcoholic who can ever hope to achieve permanent sobriety, and happiness and contentment. Many are the souls that are cast aside along life's highway simply because they are too proud to use the means that God has ordained for their rehabilitation and salvation—"He hath scattered the proud in the conceit of their heart."

At the meetings, in private conversation and discussion, wherever A.A.'s are gathered together, humility always comes in for its share of the discussion. It is the most important of the virtues, for without it there can be no true virtue. Yet, at the same time, it is one of the most elusive of all the virtues. When one thinks he is most humble he is usually farthest from possessing any semblance of humility. As one self-deceived writer pharisaically said, "If you haven't read my book on humility, you haven't read anything yet."

The simplest definition of humility is the one given by St. Theresa: "Humility is truth." Therefore its opposite, pride, is nothing but a lie, an inordinate or exaggerated opinion of one's self. That is the precise reason why an alcoholic is usually such a liar, because he is so inordinately proud; that is why the original acceptance of the A.A. Program is so difficult, because the alcoholic has so seldom admitted the truth; and finally that is why the alcoholic has become such a frustrated personality, because he has been working on false premises. Hence the first step becomes the biggest obstacle to the A.A. prospect and yet it is the most important step of the whole program. *For* without a *full* admission in the first step, the *full* practice of the subsequent steps becomes an impossibility. On the other hand, if one does *fully* admit his real condition in the first step, the other eleven become an absolute necessity. Many of the difficulties with the program stem from the fact that the individual did not or will not honestly and unequivocally admit "that he is powerless over alcohol and that his life has become unmanageable." And this is simply saying that he or she refuses to practice *humility*.

In a way it should not be so hard to admit that one is an alcoholic. If we fully understood the program and the blessings and abilities that come with it. It's something like the story of the bricklayer. One day he and his fellow worker were discussing the inequalities of life, how some seem to fare so much better than others. "Take for example yourself, Mike," Pat ruefully remarked; "You have a brother that is a Bishop, and here you are a bricklayer." "Yes," Mike replied, "it's a shame, the poor fellow couldn't lay a brick if his life depended on it."

Humility is not a denial of good qualities, for being *truth* it is the admission of *all* qualities both good and bad. We admit our faults and endeavor to remedy them; we admit our abilities, accept them as a gift of God and use them. If one is absolutely truthful in the estimation of himself, that person is humble. He accepts his good qualities, his abilities and his accomplishments as the work of God. Such a person when he comes on the program does not exclaim, "See what I have accomplished," but rather in the words of that great scientist, Samuel B. Morse, marvels at his progress with an exclamation of awe, "What God hath wrought!" His defects he clearly knows and he admits them to God, to himself and to his fellowmen. He looks forward to the elimination of them, not through his own strength or ability, but by the grace and help of a Power greater than himself, a supreme Power whom we call God. Until such an attitude of humble estimation of oneself is achieved, no one will attain contented sobriety on the program, for without humility the program is impossible. One person, after having been apparently on the program for a few weeks, slipped and became very full of self-pity—which is also from pride. He sent for his sponsor and crying on his shoulder exclaimed, "And to think I have lost all my pride!" "Swell," his sponsor bluntly remarked, "NOW we can begin."

Humility is the root of all the other virtues and hence the very cornerstone of the program.

It is the root of FAITH. For a firm belief in God demands that we take someone else's word for His attributes. We *must* be open-minded, which is but a synonym for honesty. We must accept things on the word of God; we must be willing to learn more about God; and we must admit that *God alone can restore us to sanity*. Without humility this is impossible.

It is the root of *HOPE*. The proud man trust in himself. He has no hope outside of his own puny abilities which in reality are but mere fantasies in his pride-blinded intellect. On the other hand the humble man realizes his helplessness and hopes for all things—for the guidance, for the strength and for the accomplishment—from the goodness of a merciful and omnipotent God.

It is the root of CHARITY. The humble man is good to his fellow-man. He is patient, forbearing, tolerant, for he esteems *all* men without exception his brothers under God their common Father. He ever keeps uppermost in his conscious mind, "but for the Grace of God, there go I." And he is ever on the alert to be ready—ready to be a fitting instrument in the hands of God in His Providence of Love.

It is the root of CHASTITY. The humble man realizes the need of Divine Help; he knows his inherent human weakness, and therefore he avoids the occasions of sin.

It is the root of OBEDIENCE. The humble man finds its easy to submit to authority. He knows that he is no longer running the show, that Almighty God has taken over the management of his life. Therefore no matter what circumstances or person dictate his action, he gladly accepts all authority as the voice of God—the Divine Will.

And so, with all the virtues, we find that each one is upheld, fortified and practiced only if it rests on true humility.

On the other hand, pride is the root of all of our troubles. In some way or other every difficulty or trouble we encounter stems from pride. Frustration of egoistical determinations is basic in every dissension in life—and that is pride. The proud man is truly the self-made man—and how he adores his maker! Such a man brooks no interference from God nor man, and that means *trouble*. What kind? Let's analyze a few:

1. RESENTMENTS or SELF-PITY—The number one twin enemy of all alcoholics. Someone is threatening to or has hurt *me*, and I am either—angry at them, or—sorry for myself. In a way self-pity is but resentment turned around. Resentments usually come first, build up, are completely frustrated and end in self-pity. We have a classic example of this in Judas. Remember the time that Mary Magdalen used the precious spices to anoint Christ? Judas was resentful. "We could sell this and give it to the poor." The liar! He wasn't interested in the poor, he was interested in Judas, in self, in financial gain. *He* was being hurt by this "waste." We know what was

the ultimate end of Judas. Resentment followed resentment, and finally the betrayal and the thirty pieces of silver failed to satisfy his ego—he was completely frustrated—he retreated into a morass of self-pity—and then—suicide. How different the humble man, for example, Peter. St. Peter sinned—seriously. He not only denied Christ, but "swore" that he "knew not the Man." Later he repented—he was sorry. Christ made him the head of His Church. But so was Judas sorry. The difference? Judas was sorry because *he* was hurt; Peter was sorry because he had hurt *Christ*. Judas became a suicide; Peter became a saint. Judas was *proud*; Peter was *humble*. Pride causes resentments; resentments turn into self-pity and suicide, either by the hand or by the bottle. The proud man constantly lives with the slogan, "I want what I want when I want it the way I want it; and if I don't get what I want when I want it the way I want it, then I am angry or I am sorry *for myself...Poor me!*

2. CRITICISM—The plague of every group. It stems from pride. The critical man adopts a slightly different slogan: "I don't like what or the way someone does something and I criticize—*not because it is wrong*, or because it does or will harm the *common good*, but because it is not what or the way I think it should be, and I criticize to destroy so *I can build me up*." Wives, families, and superiors could learn much from this. At the bottom of every destructive criticism is pride, vanity and self-conceit. Such people are just like buttons, "always popping off." One time such a person died, and the following remark was overheard at his wake: "Poor Jim, he won't like God!"

3. INTOLERANCE AND BIGOTRY—Something that keeps many out of A.A. and out of Religion. Their pride naively suggests: "That's no place for you, it's just a bunch of drunks;" or, "You don't want to go to Church, it's just a bunch of hypocrites." They don't realize, with their pride-distorted minds, that if this were true, they would be perfectly at home!

Pride makes men intolerant of people, whereas humility makes one intolerant only of evil itself. God hates sin, but He loves the sinner. Likewise the tolerant man, not blinded by pride, can see in all men the image of God—whether they are white or black; Catholic, Protestant, or Jew; rich or poor; drunk or sober. He knows that A.A. is not for any one class, or race, or creed, for he has finally learned the basic truth of human relationship—the Fatherhood of God and the Brotherhood of man; whereas the proud man is intolerant of other creeds, other races, other classes—not because they are wrong—but *"because they are not like ME."*

4. DIFFICULTY IN SUBMITTING TO GOD'S WILL—A common difficulty stemming from the refusal to admit that God knows best, that God knows better *than* I. Whereas the humble man in the words of Job is ever willing, "The Lord has given, the Lord has taken away; blessed be the Name of the Lord."

5. COURTING TEMPTATION—A cause of many slips. The proud man puts himself in the way of temptation because he has never *honestly* (humbly) admitted that *he is powerless*. He wants to prove to *himself* that *he* can handle the situation. A temporary member once remarked at one of the meetings, "I go into a tavern every day and drink a "coke" *to prove to myself that I don't have to take a drink of liquor."* Yes, he is still drinking—liquor. Another fellow, after one of his frequent slips, moaned, "I can't understand why I slipped; I didn't do anything but *pick up a woman and go to a tavern!"*

6. WORRY AND DESPONDENCY. Someone has defined worry as "an exaggerated sense of one's own responsibility." That's pride. Such a person forgets or refuses to admit that the outcome of every action of life is *God's responsibility*; we are responsible for only the footwork. Worry is always the property of the management, and we in A.A. have place the entire management of our lives in the hands of God. Therefore, the end results are HIS business not OURS. Of course we must plan, but not the result, only the work.

Despondency or discouragement are very akin to worry. They too stem from pride. The proud man easily becomes discouraged. Such a person does not progress as fast as he thinks he should. He thinks *his* efforts should produce results, not realizing that all success is entirely in the hands of God. We need only to make the honest effort. The great danger of despondency is, that being deceived by our pride, we become blind to the truth, and are discouraged at difficulties against which we find no strength *in ourselves*; we fail to see the Omnipotent God whose strength *can never fail*. All that is asked of us is to keep on honestly trying. God knows what a mess we are trying to untangle—but we should always remember the "when" of the untangling is in the hands of God, not ours.

7. BOASTING. We read in the A.A. book that we are to tell our story *when it is necessary to help others*. The proud man takes every

opportunity to brag of his drinking days, ever trying to top the other fellow's story. Did you ever hear, "Take me for example, *I'm* a real alcoholic—I drank two quarts a day for forty years!"

8. LACK OF CONTRITION. The proud man blames everyone and everything but himself for his troubles—nervousness, sleeplessness, heredity, environment, family, job, employer, and what have you. He is too proud to admit that for most of his difficulties *he* is to blame; that in most circumstances of life, he can't change others, but *he* can change. He has an act of contrition of his own making. "Through *your* fault" is his daily slogan. Let's don't forget Judas!

9. LACK OF SERENITY. True peace and serenity are only possible through an humble acceptance of *all* the circumstances of life as the Will of God. The proud man is ever trying to arrange *his* affairs as *he* wants them, and hence is always full of conflicts and discontentment. Let us not forget that discontentment is, in plain English, nothing else but rebellion against the Will of God.

10. SLIPS THROUGH SPIRITUAL PRIDE. Many a man has come into A.A. and made amazing progress in a very short time. Then, forgetting that all this is a gift of God, he begins to think his progress his own. He becomes like the Pharisees "who trusted in themselves and despised others." Remember the story from scripture? "Two men went up to the temple to pray, the one a Pharisee and the other a Publican. The Pharisee standing prayed thus within himself: 'O God, I give Thee thanks that I am not like the rest of men, extortioners, unjust, adulterers, as also is this Publican. I fast twice a week, I pay tithes of all I possess.' But the Publican standing afar off, would not as much as raise his eyes to heaven, but kept striking his breast saying: 'O God, be merciful to me a sinner.' I tell you, this man went back to his home justified rather than the other; for everyone who exalts himself shall be humbled, and he who humbles himself shall be exalted."

Some time ago I had occasion to come face to face with a striking example of spiritual pride. One of the members of a group was condemning certain ones for their failure to do what he thought they ought to do. Then, "Take *me* for example, I go to Communion every morning, I teach my children Catechism—in fact I have arrived at a point *where anything I make up my mind to do I can do it*." Strewing incense at his own shrine. Stupidly glorifying himself. The sequel? He's still drunk.

The longer we are sober the more it becomes necessary to keep ever in our conscious mind, "I am what I am *by the grace of God.* Isn't it marvelous that God can do so much with such poor material?" Remember vice will always beget vice, but *vainglory* alone is begotten of virtue.

Examples of difficulties and troubles stemming from pride are endless. On the other hand the rewards of humility are unlimited. We find the perfect *expression* of this in the reply which the Blessed Virgin Mary gave the Angel Gabriel when he told her she was to become the Mother of Christ. It is called the "Magnificat;"

"My soul doth magnify the Lord,

And my spirit hath rejoiced in God my Savior,

Because He hath regarded the humility of His handmaid;

For behold henceforth all generations shall call me blessed..."

The greatest honor bestowed upon a member of the human race—"The Mother of God"—was given "because He hath regarded the *humility* of His handmaid."

"For *He that is Mighty* hath done great things to me, and holy is His name"...Not see what *I have done,* but *"What God has wrought."*

And His mercy is from generation unto generations to them that fear Him.

"He hath showed might in His arm; *He hath scattered the proud in the conceit of their heart"*...The former A.A.'s who are drinking again have been "scattered in the conceit of their heart!"

"He hath put down *the mighty from their seat"*...the mighty in their own estimation. The "I can do it on my own-ers."

"He hath *exalted the humble"*...Take a look at the ones who are humbly working the program...the serenity, the happiness, the success...

"He hath filled *the hungry with good things"*...Those who *admitted they* were powerless, who were hungry for the help of God...

"And *the rich he hath sent empty away"*...Did you ever hear them? "I haven't lost my job, I've got money, I've got my family, I don't need A.A."

The perfect *example* of humility is Christ. Follow Him through His life, His passion, His death. Heed His words, "Learn of Me, for I am meek and *humble* of heart."

In the A.A. book we read, "As we go through the day, we pause when agitated or doubtful, and ask for the right thought or action. We constantly reminded ourselves many times each day 'Thy Will be done'... that we are no longer running the show...we are then in much less danger of excitement, fear, anger, worry, self-pity, criticism, or foolish decisions. We become more efficient...humbly abandon yourself to God ... admit your faults to Him and your fellowman ... it works, it really does."

A retreat master once said:

"The price of real maturity in life is a realization of the mistakes we have made. You young men will be really mature the day you look back on your life and cry out: "My God, what a mess I've made of things!" That day will be a great day for you, but it will be a day, too, when only a *real deep humility* will enable you, despite the mess of the past, to go forward and do life's work."

"It is easy enough, in the years when life's blood is coursing through our veins to rush on and on from day to day, from week to week, and even from year to year taking each new task in its stride... but then sooner or later—unless we fail to learn humility—the day of awakening comes...it may come with a blinding flash that seems to tear away the very foundations of life...but it must come if we are ever to be mature... My God, what a mess I've made of things! As I look back how pitiful is the good done, how sparing my help to others, how innumerable my mistakes, the wrongs, how all-pervading my self-seeking! How seamy the finished product!"

"Is such a realization discouraging? Absolutely, unless—unless I fall on my knees and *humbly* admit it all to God, with a heartfelt thanks that He knows and understands and will make allowance, full allowance, for my pitiful human frailty. What else could He—or I—expect? Then from my knees I arise and face the future, trusting far less in myself than ever before, and throwing my full weight on God, *knowing that it will be an easy burden for omnipotence.*"

HOW ABOUT IT?

AN INTERPRETATION OF
THE TWELVE STEPS

1. WE ADMITTED WE WERE POWERLESS OVER ALCOHOL—THAT OUR LIVES HAD BECOME UNMANAGEABLE.

This is first of all an *admission*—an act of the mind. It is not something calling for strength of *will*, but something that calls for a weakening of a rebellious will—an honest *admission*—a *giving in*—or in plain language a true act of *humility* which is nothing more nor less than absolute honesty. The objective fact that we are powerless perhaps has been there for years, but now we recognize that fact, we *admit it*—we take the first step on the road to honesty and humility which alone can lead to sobriety and happiness.

We admit that we are *powerless*. In the matter of alcohol we have absolutely no control, no will. The statements that are made so often by many well-meaning persons about the alcoholic's willpower being rejuvenated is a lot of nonsense. It is this fallacy that leads many after a period of sobriety to "try it again." Experience proves beyond a doubt that an alcoholic can *never* hope to "rejuvenate" his willpower and again control his drinking—he is *powerless*. He has *no will in the matter of alcohol*.

It was quite interesting to read some time ago about an alcoholic who lived in Dublin, Ireland, in the early part of this century. His name is Matt Talbott. For sixteen years he drank heavily. Finally he came, as we say, to his level. *He made up his mind to do something* about his drinking and turned to God for the solution. Through the grace of God he not only remained sober, but for forty years led a very holy and penitential life. Today the cause for his Canonization has been introduced at Rome, and we hope that, in God's Providence, he will be canonized. If and when he is, it will be the first alcoholic that the Catholic Church will have canonized.

It is stated in his biography that he came to realize that in the matter of alcohol *he had no will*. Therefore, as a matter of desperate necessity, he had to turn to Almighty God Who alone could give him permanent sobriety. But all the time he was very conscious of the fact that never again could he ever hope to drink normally. Now this is exactly what we mean when we admit we are *powerless—we have no will in the matter of alcoholic indulgence*—and the strength to remain sober must come from the outside, from Almighty God, a fact we shall consider in the next step.

"Admitted we were powerless *over alcohol*." That is very plain.

Alcohol means *all* alcohol: beer, wine, or what have you. No "beer experiment' or 'wine experiment'—unless you want to learn the hard way. If you are not fully convinced of this, a little beer will convince you—very dramatically! But we prefer to accept the universal experience which tells us that when we say we are powerless over *alcohol*, we mean *all* alcohol—period.

"That our lives had become unmanageable." We admit that we have drifted away from *normal* living, normal thinking, normal drinking. Anyone who will stop a moment to analyze one of his 'binges' should not have a very difficult time admitting that he has drifted away from normalcy. Certainly normal people don't act the way we invariably did on our binges.

We further admit that we have tried innumerable methods to live, think *and drink* normally—and always failed. We tried medicine, psychiatry, etc., and they didn't seem to work. So we have come to a point where we admit that in the managing of our lives we are a complete failure. Again honesty—humility. We *are alcoholic.*

Now at this point come the questions that are much discussed in the meetings: "What is an alcoholic?;" "Am I an alcoholic?"

You have heard some remark that they drank two quarts a day. I never will forget the first meeting that I attended. It so happened that an A.A. from out of town was there and made the very positive statement, "I drank two quarts a day for years!"—it scared the daylights out of me! Now, after a bit of experience in the group, I have a slight suspicion that when one says he drank two quarts a day for years—he is bragging. It certainly is by no means necessary to have drunk so much to be a true alcoholic. It is not even necessary to have drunk daily. Perhaps we needed a drink the next morning, perhaps we did not; perhaps we drank alone, perhaps we didn't; maybe we drank constantly, maybe only periodically. In my opinion, I do not believe any of these factors has any bearing on whether one is an alcoholic or not. For years one person went on the fallacy that when one drank the next morning then and then only was he to be considered an alcoholic. The innumerable days he fought with bromides, aspirin, barbitals, etc., etc., just to avoid that morning drink! But come noon—he could drink to his heart's content and not be an alcoholic!

What then *is* an alcoholic? I believe the most all-inclusive definition of an alcoholic is: One who having taken *one* drink, cannot absolutely guarantee his behavior; one to whom drinking has become a major problem in his life. It makes little difference how often we drink, how long we drink, or where, when, why or how we drink, *if drinking has become a major problem in our life we are alcoholic.* And being an alcoholic we know that we cannot take that *first* drink. If we do, the problem of drinking to us will become progressively worse, will bring innumerable other problems in its train, and our lives again will become unmanageable. The end? Insanity or death.

Sincerity and honesty in making this admission in the first step is half the solution. Many slip because somewhere in the back of their minds they retain the false hope that maybe some day, somehow, they again will be able to drink normally. Then that supposed day comes—a drink—and bang, off to the races! One who *fully* takes the first step—once and for all—will *want* and *practice* the other eleven. But one who takes it with some sort of a mental reservation, a mental 'maybe,' will only half-heartedly, if at all, practice the others. To *honestly* and *completely* admit that we are powerless over alcohol—that our lives have become unmanageable is the only door that opens to the Alcoholics Anonymous program.

NOTES

2. CAME TO BELIEVE THAT A POWER GREATER THAN OURSELVES COULD RESTORE US TO SANITY.

"A Power greater than ourselves," i.e., a Power outside and beyond *human* power, the Power which we call *God*. We have tried medicine and many other ways and methods to no avail, so now we are going to try the spiritual. This is not religion. Religion is the *formal* worship of God, and has nothing to do with A.A. nor does A.A. have anything to do with religion. The second step simply means that we came to believe that there is a God, and that God can restore us to normal and happy living. We do not approach this step with an attitude of 'show me,' but with an humble attitude of acceptance, an attitude of faith and humility—with an open mind, willing to learn more about this Power Whom we call God. If a person *won't* admit this, he is rather hopeless and A.A. has little, if anything, to offer. For, the person who refuses to accept the fact that there is anything, or any Power, greater than himself, is rather a hopeless egotist. To his stinted mind, no thing, no person, not even a God can do something more than he in his blinding pride thinks he can do.

However, we do find people who want the A.A. program (and need it!) who *can't* seem to accept the idea of God. There is here a big difference from the one who *won't* accept it. The former is sincere, honest and willing. And in the course of time—in God's own time—such a person will be enabled by the grace of God to see clearly. Experience has borne out this fact time and time again. But the man who *positively refuses* to believe in God hasn't a chance as long as he retains such negative attitude and bad will. It is clearly stated in the Alcoholic Anonymous book that "No one should have difficulty with the spiritual side of the program. *Willingness, honesty and open-mindedness are essentials* of recovery. But they *are indispensable!*"

One man solved his difficulties in this manner: "I've thought a lot about the idea of God, and I found it difficult to believe in God. However, I finally reasoned it out this way—When I die I would rather wake up in the next life finding there is no God, having believed in Him here, than to find there is a God, having *not* believed in Him here." That is very logical.

We find by experience that the firmer and greater our belief in God the greater will be our success in sobriety, the greater our happiness and the more serene our contentment. The more fully we admit that God, and God alone can restore us to sanity, the more will we seek God as the solution of *all* of our problems and difficulties; and the more willing will we be to make the full decision to turn our life and will over to Him as we do in the third step.

NOTES

3. MADE A DECISION TO TURN OUR WILL AND OUR LIVES OVER TO THE CARE OF GOD *AS WE UNDERSTOOD HIM*.

This is another decision—a *full* decision with no reservations, no holding back, no 'ifs,' 'and' or 'buts.' The more complete and unconditional our decision was in step number one, the more readily and fully will we make this decision to turn our lives over to God. It is the mental reservations in the admission that we are powerless over alcohol and that our lives have become unmanageable that often proves a stumbling block in step number three. Many would like to turn *most* of their lives over to the care of God, but certain associations, practices, and relationships—we don't like to let them go. But we should realize that, when we make up our minds to turn our will and our lives over to the care of God, that means without reservation. Therefore all dishonesty, dishonest practices, illicit relationships, and all the many things in our lives *that we know are contrary to the will of God must go*. It is here that we understand fully the meaning of the term "unconditional surrender." And having once and for all fully made this decision of surrender, we will, perhaps for the first time in our lives, experience the true meaning of peace and serenity. We will finally really begin to live. We shall at last understand what Christ meant when He told us that we must die in order to live—die to all that is of self in order to live to all that is of God—His will, His providence, His Love.

If we are not willing to take this step unconditionally, then as we are advised in the A.A. book, we should pray that God will make us willing—praying both for the will to do and the strength to accomplish. This, for a time, may be necessary for most of us. For, after years away from normal living, from God and His will, it is not going to be so easy to change and we may need to pray daily, even hourly, "God, make me willing to do Thy will."

"As we understood Him." We are above everything else searching for *truth*. Therefore, we don't *make up* a God to fit *us*, but we search for God *according to our honest convictions*. We want a God Who "can restore us to sanity," a "Power greater than ourselves," not a figment of *our* imagination or a product of *our* own will. If we have no clear cut idea of God, we *ask* that *He* give it to us. Isn't it very plain that the making of a God to suit *us* is a contradiction of the admission we make "that *we were powerless*"? The safe and sure way is to *humbly* pray, "God, that I may see!"

NOTES

4. MADE A SEARCHING AND FEARLESS MORAL INVENTORY OF OURSELVES.

"Searching and fearless." 'To search' means to *carefully* look for. "Fearless" means having no fear of *whatever* we may find. Therefore, when we make a "searching and fearless inventory," we are going to leave *no* nook nor cranny of ourselves, past or present, unturned. We are going to *fearlessly search* for *all* of our defects. We are not going to make a phony list; we have been making such a list for years, and now we are going to replace it with an honest one—item by item. We do not find any successful business man taking an inventory and making wild guesses as to the actual kind and number of his stock in trade. Imagine such a person looking on his shelves and saying: "*About* a dozen of such-and-such," missing half of them. No; he takes his stock item by item. How many of this? Twelve. How many of that? Sixteen—ten good, six spoiled. Of course we are going to find a lot of rotten stock, but then what do we expect to find after years of abnormal living and drinking? Some of it is going to be a little putrid and unpleasant, *but it is in the inventory*. That is the basic reason we are taking it—in order to know what has to be eliminated in the next step. They tell of the gentleman who came to his sponsor with twenty one typewritten pages! He was honest, he knew the real meaning of the terms "searching and fearless;" and he got in return happiness and peace and serenity.

Now we come to the question, "What measuring stick are we to use in taking our inventory?" In other words how are we going to know what is to be eliminated from the stock at hand?

First we have CONSCIENCE. Every human being has been endowed by his Creator with a basic knowledge of good and evil. The alcoholic, who probably has subjected his conscience to a false justification of his antics, should of course precede his inventory with humble prayer for guidance. Again, "O God that I may see!"

Next we have the TEN COMMANDMENTS of God. They point out definite actions, etc., which are right or wrong. They show us our obligations to God and to our fellowman. They both command and forbid—they are the positive Divine measuring rod.

Then there are the OBLIGATIONS OF OUR STATE OF LIFE as a married man, a father of a family, a man in business, and all the obligations which we assumed by the particular circumstances in which we live.

We also may have OBLIGATIONS TO OUR CHURCH. In this there are specific obligations as to attendance, church laws, etc.

Again we have the SEVEN FUNDAMENTAL PASSIONS of man: The tendency to pride, envy, greed, lust, gluttony, sloth, and anger (which includes that A-1 enemy of all alcoholics—resentment). What are we going to do about these? Those who are experienced in such matters tell us that we should "act contrary." Therefore, if we tend to be angry and resentful, we should practice the contrary positive act by speaking kindly and doing good to those against whom we are angry or resentful. This *positive* act will tend to eliminate the negative angry feeling or tendency. If we tend to be greedy, we should practice the charity of giving; if we tend to be slothful (which is nothing else but plain laziness) we should endeavor to keep busy; and so on down the list. We do not *worry* about them, nor about getting rid of them, for we shall have them more or less all of our lives. Our job is simply to try *daily* to control them. The ultimate elimination of them is in the hands of God.

If we analyze the human being, we shall find that the mind or soul is a simple substance and can not be divided. This is the reason that in our drinking days we were always so unhappy and so full of conflicts. We were doing things secretly and trying not to do them publicly. This can't be done, for the soul of man is indivisible. We can use this truth to great advantage in fighting against our evil tendencies. If we pick out our biggest failing, our most frequent tendency to evil, and work on that one the rest will come along. Therefore, if we *daily* strive with the help of God to control our *predominant passion*, all the other passions will take care of themselves. But again, we don't ask ourselves how are we doing, but how are we trying. We have only the footwork to do, the success is up to God.

Lastly we have the opposites of the three fundamental virtues:

The opposite of *Faith* is FEAR. Fear is a vacillation of the mind. The "prop" of Faith is loose. To eliminate fear we make acts of Faith in God, in our fellowman and in ourselves. And then we *act on this Faith* in God, in our fellowman and in ourselves. We *practice* it. "If God be with us who can be against us? If God be with us, whom shall we fear?"

The opposite of *Hope* is DESPAIR. Despair begins in self-pity. It has its roots in self-centeredness. Hence we should divert our gaze from ourselves, and look to God. We should put complete trust and absolute confidence in His Power, His mercy, and His love.

The opposite of *Love* is HATRED. Hatred for our fellowman comes from a lack of realization that *all* men are children of God our Father. Therefore, if we truly love God and our fellowman, there will be no room for hatred. even for the lowest of His creatures.

"Of *ourselves*." We in no way permit the faults of others to enter this inventory. We assume full responsibility. It is an inventory of ourselves and *our* faults, not of our wives, nor of our boss, nor of our family, nor of our friends—it is *a searching and fearless moral inventory of ourselves.*

NOTES

5. ADMITTED TO GOD, TO OURSELVES, AND TO ANOTHER HUMAN BEING THE EXACT NATURE OF OUR WRONGS.

First of all this step implies that we have sorrow for what we have done wrong, and that *we* admit that *we* have been responsible for it. This is not self-pity or self-sorrow. It is sorrow that we have hurt or offended God and our fellowman, *not that we have been hurt*. We have been loaded with self-pity for years and now, by admitting *our fault* to God, to ourselves and to another human being, we are going to go far in eliminating sorrow for self.

We see the big difference between true sorrow and self-pity in St. Peter and Judas. Judas was sorry, and Peter was sorry, but Judas was sorry because *he had been hurt*, "he repented *himself.*" Thus he became full of self-pity, which in turn led to despair and suicide. Peter was sorry because he had denied *Christ*. Peter had contrition, Judas nothing but self-pity.

By no means should we permit ourselves to fumble around in a morass of self-pity, or what is as bad, indulge in self-condemnation. If we do we are liable to start a guilt-complex and our state will be worse than before. We shall be of no use to ourselves nor anybody else.

"We admitted to *ourselves.*" This means that we admitted that *we* are responsible—that all the mess we are in, *we* could have avoided it. For once in our lives we begin to accept responsibility.

"Admitted...to *another human being.*" Some might hold back at this, thinking that the admission to God and to themselves is sufficient. But let's remember—we are alcoholics, we want not only sobriety but peace and contentment, and we *need big chunks of humility*. Holding back from this step is nothing more nor less than being too *proud* to let someone else know how loaded we are with faults and failings. It is very indicative that the admission to God and to ourselves was not very honest, and came not from the heart but merely from the lips.

In regard to Catholics they will want to go to confession, but that is not enough, they should have a full discussion of their soul's condition with their confessor, in order that they might receive proper advice and direction in eliminating the *cause* of the wrongs they confess. A non-Catholic may go to anyone he chooses, but all should remember that, if it is to be to a member of the group, it should be with *one who has taken this step*, not with someone who might say, "I never took that step, and look at me, I'm sober." Such a one may be sober *now*, but experience proves that *no one* will achieve contentment and happiness and serenity *unless* they admit their faults to *another human being*. It is the doing of this all-important job that casts our fears, phobias, and dishonesty. And having completed it, we can at last face the world, and anyone in that world, with a clear conscience and a serenity that must be experienced to be understood.

"We admitted...the *exact* nature of our wrongs." Again we have honesty. Nothing counts but being honest. No dressing up, no cutting corners, but thoroughly, and honestly and *exactly* admitting the nature of our wrongs. "It works, it really does!"

NOTES

6. WERE ENTIRELY READY TO HAVE GOD REMOVE ALL THESE DEFECTS OF CHARACTER.

We are *ready* and *willing*. We place everything in the hands of God. We are willing to let His Providence work on our character in order to rebuild it. He may use some striking measures, but we are ready. He may put us in circumstances where someone is always aggravating us—that is to teach us *patience*. He may give us association with someone we don't like—that is to teach us *charity* and *tolerance*. He may put us in a position of inferiority—that is to teach us *humility*. He may bring it about that we have to work hard—that is to eliminate *laziness*. He may even give us failure—that is to teach us *courage* and *trust in Him*. All the disappointments, circumstances or whatever He may arrange for us in His Providence, are *all* going to be opportunities to eliminate our defect of character.

The present Archbishop of Indianapolis made a statement shortly after he was appointed to the Archdiocese that fits in exactly with what his step implies. Some of the priests of the Archdiocese called on him to find out what arrangements he wanted to make for his installation as Archbishop. He told them, "You go ahead and make the arrangements, I'll fit in." Now that is what we are saying to Almighty God, "You arrange my life. I have turned it over to Your Providence. *I'll fit in.* Grant me the grace to change the things I can; to accept the things I cannot change; and the wisdom to know the difference." But in *all* things, *Thy will be done!*

NOTES

7. HUMBLY ASKED HIM TO REMOVE OUR SHORTCOMINGS.

Again we have humility. Realizing that the job we are ready to undertake is humanly impossible, we ask Him to do it for us and give us the strength to do the footwork. We cannot ask Him *once* and then quit—we ask Him *daily*. We cannot ask for the morrow, only for today—twenty-four hours at a time, more often if necessary. It is normally a slow process, this rejuvenation of our character and personality. But after all, we did not get this way overnight, and we are not going to come into full personality overnight. It is ordinarily a lifetime work. We should always remember that we are working on the most difficult job in life—we are rebuilding, not a house, nor a town, nor a nation, nor a world, but a *man*. That is slow. It is difficult, and we should never be agitated over lack of progress. If we get mad again, if we become resentful, or if all of our faults pop back on occasion, we are not surprised, but are amazed that we don't do worse. As long as we are honestly doing the footwork, hand in hand with Almighty God, we know that in His own time, success will be ours—a *gift* from God.

NOTES

8. MADE A LIST OF ALL PERSONS WE HAD HARMED, AND BECAME WILLING TO MAKE AMENDS TO THEM ALL.

"Made a *list*"—a list of the people *we had harmed*. Why a list? So that seeing these injustices, black on white, they may be the more emphatically impressed on our minds and memories. It is to replace a list that we have carried around in our imaginations for years of the people who, so we thought, were *harming us*. We had resentfully gone along imagining that if we could only change circumstances, we would change; that if people would only change, we would change; that *if we could change others,* we would be all right. As one person remarked, "If you would only make my wife change, I'd be O.K." Nonsense! We can't often change others, but *we* can change—*we* can *"fit in."* And, in making an *honest* list in this step, we are amazed to find that it wasn't others who were harming us, but that *we* had been harming others.

"Made a list of *all* the persons we had harmed." Honestly again. We leave out *no one* from this list. Whether friend or foe, whether we like them or not, whether superior or inferior, we make a list of *all* the persons we had harmed. We make no excuses in the odd case where we had also been harmed; we don't say, "Well, maybe I did harm him, but after all look what he did to me"—no 'buts,' no self-exoneration, no retaliation—*all* the persons *we* had harmed. Difficult? Sure, but only unbending egotism makes it impossible.

"The persons we had *harmed*." Our injustices will be classified under three heads: *Material* wrongs; *Moral* wrongs; and *Spiritual* wrongs.

MATERIAL. The wrongs we have done others in matters of material things: money, damages, injury to persons and property, and any injustice in the material order.

MORAL. The injuries we have done to others wherein we have been the direct or indirect cause of his wrongdoings. We have given scandal; led others to wrongdoing by bad example to friends, associates, family, etc.; taught others to do wrong, to drink, steal, etc.; permitted others to drift into evil ways by shirking responsibilities to children, inferiors, etc.

SPIRITUAL. The wrongs we have done by neglect of our obligations to our Church and our God; neglect of prayer and the worship owing to God. Here we find the necessity of penance for *all* our wrongs, over and above the mere restitutions owing in justice and indicated under material and moral wrongs.

"Became willing to make amends to them *all*." We are willing and *ready*. No hesitancy and still no hurry. We take our time in order to be thorough. We have agreed to *go to any length* to defeat alcohol, therefore we are ready to make amends to them *all*—even our enemies!

NOTES

9. MADE DIRECT AMENDS TO SUCH PEOPLE WHEREVER POSSIBLE, EXCEPT WHEN TO DO SO WOULD INJURE THEM OR OTHERS.

"Made *direct* amends." This may seem and actually be difficult, especially to people we don't like, but we have asked for it. We want humility and we know that an alcoholic needs humility more than anything else in the world. This step is a short cut to humility. Ordinarily, if a person has done an injustice, he may make it up without the injured person's knowledge. In such manner he has fulfilled his obligation *of justice*, but he has not practiced *humility*. When we are asked or advised to make amends directly and openly to the ones we have harmed, we are simply being shown the shortest route to the practice of humility. Hence we admit our faults and make restitution *openly* and *directly* to the persons we have harmed. We don't do it in a 'behind the bush' manner—we make *direct* amends.

"Wherever *possible*." We don't hedge in this matter of making restitution, but in some instances it is either impossible or in the doing of it we would injure *others*. In such cases, under *competent* advice, we turn the matter over to God. This is often the only recourse in matters of scandal where we can only through our prayers and sacrifices humbly petition God to make up to the person we had led to wrongdoing.

Some don't like this idea of leaving it up to God. We wish we could make it up. We fail to see the pride that lies hidden in such desire. Or else our weak faith fails to realize that the omnipotent God, on Whom we are relying to restore us to sanity and sobriety, can and will make up all the damage in such cases *if we have the humility to leave it in His hands*. Pride says, "I wish *I* could make it up"; humility admits, "I can't, God. You do it for me."

So, in circumstances we can't change; instances where we might do serious harm to others; and in cases where restitution is *impossible*, we place it entirely in the hands of God. But in all of these circumstances, we only do so *on competent advice*. We never trust our own judgment. That is one of the purposes of the discussion of our faults and wrongs with another.

"Injure *them* or *others*." We take no thought of any possible or even probable injury that might come *to us* in this step. We hesitate only *when* we might injure *others*. It may even be that we might suffer serious inconvenience and have our standing seriously hurt, but "we agreed to go to any length to defeat alcohol." If we haven't, we had better go back to step one and begin over again—*honestly*.

This business of restitution may take a long time. It may even takes years, but it is thoroughness, not haste, that counts. We do not hurry, *nor* do we *needlessly* delay. "Easy does it," but *procrastination* is very destructive of honesty and sincerity.

NOTES

10. CONTINUED TO TAKE PERSONAL INVENTORY AND WHEN WE WERE WRONG PROMPTLY ADMITTED IT.

Here we have a continuation of steps four, eight, and nine. When we took our general inventory we had quite a shock. We thought we had a good business, that we were big shots, that *we* didn't have any faults; but when we took stock honestly, we found to our dismay that we weren't much at all and that all the virtues we thought we possessed were falsely labeled. Now we do not intend to have this happen again, so we regularly (daily if possible) take an honest personal inventory As mentioned previously, in this inventory we don't pay too much attention to *how* we have succeeded, but only to how honestly we are *trying*. The success is up to God, ours is only the footwork. This conviction will help to avoid indulging in self-pity with some such soliloquy as "I have tried so hard for so long and I still get angry, get hurt, criticize, etc." What do we expect? We should be amazed that we don't do worse. We should always remember that God in judgment is not going to ask how much we have accomplished, but *how honestly and sincerely* did we *try*. And the strongest and the weakest can always sincerely try.

"*Personal* inventory." This is to prevent a relapse into the old fallacy of thinking that others were injuring us. If we strive for a constant and true knowledge of *ourselves*, we won't be so apt to blame others or to judge them. This is a *personal* inventory—*our* faults.

There is one great danger in this regular inventory. When we look for our faults we might concentrate too much on our progress and fall into what we call 'spiritual pride.' For if, through God's grace, we are enabled to eliminate many of our faults, we are liable to take the credit to ourselves, which is pride again and the prelude to a bad collapse. Like the person mentioned in our discussion of humility,[1] we can so easily take the attitude of "See what *I* have accomplished," instead of the humble admiration of "What *God* has wrought." Many of us have miraculously eliminated certain faults *by the grace of God*. And by ever being conscious of the fact that it is *God's Work*, not ours, we shall avoid the pitfall of spiritual pride. God, in His mercy, often permits many faults to remain—in order to keep us humble.

---

1. Cf. Humility—p. 26.

"When wrong *promptly* admitted it." We don't find excuses or, by pure procrastination, put it off, but we make it up (whatever the wrong may be) *immediately*. Why? Because if we don't, we probably will begin to think the other person was at fault, and resentment will set in, grow and bear fruit—discontent, negative thinking, neglect of prayer and—a little drink might lift our spirits! Remember?

NOTES

11. SOUGHT THROUGH PRAYER AND MEDITATION TO IMPROVE OUR CONSCIOUS CONTACT WITH GOD *AS WE UNDERSTOOD HIM,* PRAYING ONLY FOR KNOWLEDGE OF HIS WILL FOR US AND THE POWER TO CARRY THAT OUT.

We analyze this step in our discussion of prayer and meditation.[1] However we should bear four things always in mind:

1) We must *seek*. We must make an honest effort to learn to pray well and to meditate well—*daily*.

2) We must seek *to improve* our *conscious* contact with God. We cannot stagnate and accept whatever idea of God happens to be ours at the beginning of our sobriety. We must *with an open mind* seek *to improve*, and gradually become more and more *God-conscious*.

3) We must pray for *knowledge of God's will*, not that God will satisfy *our wills*. "Illumine my mind, inflame my heart, strengthen my will!" *"Thy* will be done!"

4) We must *ask* for the *strength* which will constantly remind us that *we are powerless*. And, since we need this Divine assistance daily, we must *daily* ask God for it.

---
1. Cf. p. 7.

NOTES

12. HAVING HAD A SPIRITUAL AWAKENING AS THE RESULT OF THESE STEPS, WE TRIED TO CARRY THIS MESSAGE TO ALCOHOLICS, AND TO PRACTICE THESE PRINCIPLES IN ALL OUR AFFAIRS.

"A spiritual *experience* or *awakening*." Many are stumped by this. After a period of sobriety, they can't seem to realize that they have had any spiritual experience or awakening. The reason is because many do not understand what the expression signifies. If they would ask themselves: "Who sent someone to explain A.A.? Who enabled me to remain sober for the time I have been dry in spite of frequent craving and temptation? Who enabled me to pray these past weeks or months? Who brought about all of the entire chain of circumstances that brought me to the condition of sobriety I enjoy today? I admitted I was powerless, where did the strength come from?" *God gave it to me.* Each and every circumstance that helped me along the road to sobriety was the *experiencing of Spiritual help*—the help of God, a spiritual experience. And, as a result, we have *awakened* to a new sense of values, new attitudes towards life, God, and our fellowman—in short we have had a *spiritual awakening*.

Many seem to have great difficulty in achieving this awakening. Those who have such difficulty might well *carefully* retrace the other eleven steps, for in step twelve we have the spiritual awakening *as a result of these steps*. And anyone who does not have this spiritual rebirth and *know* it in all probability has not *honestly* and *thoroughly* taken the first eleven steps, for when they have thus taken them, no one will have to tell them; they *will* have the spiritual awakening and *they will know it*. Each step gives a bit—these are the spiritual experiences. They in turn contribute to the whole which is a spiritual awakening to a new life, the life of grace, of peace, and happiness and serenity. It is not our own work, but *a gift of God*, a reward for our good will and humility. "He hath regarded the humility of his handmaid...He hath exalted the humble."

"Try to *carry this message to other alcoholics*"—the so-called 'Twelfth Step Work." We do it out of a sense of gratitude and of our realization of the need of insurance against a slip. In all of the work of the twelfth step we *give*. We should always remember that the program is essentially a *give* program. We shall receive much, but not unless we give. "Freely have you received, freely give."

Let us consider some of the instances of twelfth step work:

1) We attend meetings *regularly*. This is especially necessary to keep our thinking straight and to insure against a possible let-up on the other steps with the inevitable result, a slip. Many a one has admitted that the first step toward a slip was the missing of the meetings. His insurance lapsed, he got back into his old ways of thinking—and *drinking*. We should never forget that every meeting we attend, *even though* we think *we* do not benefit by the talk, etc., we are *giving* someone a good example and encouragement by our very presence.

2) We make calls on new members *when* we are asked, not only when we *feel* like it. We are practicing charity and unselfishness—vital virtues especially for the alcoholic.

3) We speak at the meetings when asked. It is a part of our contribution. Even though we may not be accomplished public speakers, *everyone* has a message and *our* presentation may have the answer someone has been seeking for a long time.

4) We give financial donations when asked. It is amusing how 'tight' some become on the occasion of a donation being asked. Some who spend hundreds of dollars on liquor, 'squawk' their heads off when asked for fifty cents for the 'kitty.'

5) We own and loan the A.A. book. Many do not have a full knowledge of the program because they have never, or at most only cursorily, read the A.A. book. We should read and re-read it. We certainly do not absorb it in one reading. Some are amazed at certain statements made at the meetings, or in conversation, relative to the alcoholic problem and its solution which was merely taken, sometimes 'verbatim,' from the A.A. book. We should *own* the book, *read* the book, and *loan* it to others—it is all part of the twelfth step work.

6) We should encourage those with difficulties and have the patience and charity to listen to their troubles. We should never forget the day when a good listener was a necessity to us when we first came to A.A.

7) We should serve as chairmen and on the various committees when asked to do so. This is also twelfth step work and a wonderful training in both responsibility and unselfishness.

8) We should gladly sponsor new prospects and *conscientiously* accept such responsibility. There has been many a slip because the sponsor was a 'one-call-that's-all' A.A. We should realize that the average newcomer needs someone to lean on for awhile-some more, some less—until his thinking clears and he gets both feet on the program. A drowning man needs more than a throwline to save him. "Freely have you received, freely *give*."

9) Finally we should give of whatever talent we may have been blessed in order that, through us God may bring others from the darkness of alcoholic fantasy into the light of His grace.

We should do all of these things with a *conscious* idea of sacrifice in order to discipline ourselves away from the habits of selfishness into habits of unselfishness and love. We should, in fine, *work* the program and then we will never need a program for the work at hand.

NOTES

THE TWELVE STEPS

1. We admitted we were powerless over alcohol—that our lives had become unmanageable.

2. Came to believe that a Power greater than ourselves could restore us to sanity.

3. Made a decision to turn our will and our lives over to the care of God *as we understood Him.*

4. Made a searching and fearless moral inventory of ourselves.

5. Admitted to God, to ourselves, and to another human being the exact nature of our wrongs.

6. Were entirely ready to have God remove all these defects of character.

7. Humbly asked Him to remove our shortcomings.

8. Made a list of all persons we had harmed, and became willing to make amends to them all.

9. Made direct amends to such people wherever possible, except when to do so would injure them or others.

10. Continued to take personal inventory and when we were wrong promptly admitted it.

11. Sought through prayer and meditation to improve our conscious contact with God *as we understood Him,* praying only for knowledge of His will for us and the power to carry that out.

12. Having had a spiritual experience as the result of these steps, we tried to carry this message to alcoholics, and to practice these principles in all our affairs.

About Hazelden Publishing

As part of the Hazelden Betty Ford Foundation, Hazelden Publishing offers both cutting-edge educational resources and inspirational books. Our print and digital works help guide individuals in treatment and recovery, and their loved ones. Professionals who work to prevent and treat addiction also turn to Hazelden Publishing for evidence-based curricula, digital content solutions, and videos for use in schools, treatment programs, correctional programs, and electronic health records systems. We also offer training for implementation of our curricula.

Through published and digital works, Hazelden Publishing extends the reach of healing and hope to individuals, families, and communities affected by addiction and related issues.

For more information about Hazelden publications,
please call **800-328-9000**
or visit us online at **hazelden.org/bookstore.**